7 DAYS OF FASTING FOR ALIGNMENT & OVERFLOW
Healing the Heart to Make Room for Abundance

Precious Dear
Holistic Wellness Coach & Nurse Leader

COPYRIGHT PAGE

© 2025 Precious Dear
All rights reserved.

No part of this book may be reproduced, stored in a retrieval system, or transmitted in any form or by any means, electronic, mechanical, photocopying, recording, or otherwise, without prior written permission from the publisher, except in the case of brief quotations used in articles or reviews.

ISBN: 979-8-9939652-0-8
Printed in the United States of America

Precious Holistic Touch LLC
www.PreciousHolisticTouch.com

Scripture quotations are from the Holy Bible (KJV, NIV, or translation of your choice). All rights reserved by their respective publishers.

DEDICATION PAGE

To the God who aligned my steps, restored my heart, and revealed that it's all connected. This book is my yes.

TABLE OF CONTENTS

Introduction 7

Day 1 — Your Gift Makes Room for You 11

Day 2 — The Irrevocable Call 17

Day 3 — The Power to Create Wealth 23

Day 4 — Divine Insight & God-Led Vision 29

Day 5 — Seek First the Kingdom 35

Day 6 — Obedience, Capacity & Preparedness 41

Day 7 — Abundance in Every Good Work 47

Closing: Prayer, Reflection & Declaration 53

Meet the Author 62

INTRODUCTION

"I remain confident of this: I will see the goodness of the Lord in the land of the living."
— *Psalm 27:13*

For the past several months, I have walked through a season marked by stretching, sacrifice, and silent battles. A season of deficit. Overdraft notices. Declines. "Below balance" messages. Rising costs. Unending responsibility. A season where I carried the weight of being a mother, provider, student, nurse leader, visionary, caretaker, and servant of God, all at once.

And yet through it all, something holy remained constant: **I never went without.**

In every moment of pressure, God revealed Himself to me as **Jehovah Jireh**, the God who provides.
He showed up unexpectedly, creatively, faithfully:

• In the quiet generosity of my Superman, my father, sending support "just because," and through my Mother, whose motto is "if I have it you won't go without".
• In divine downloads: marketing ideas, course outlines, content prompts, and business strategies.
• Through donations and community support poured into my business and nonprofit.
• In the unwavering strength of My Honey, whose love and provision filled in every gap.

Every gesture, every ounce of support, every unexpected blessing carried the same whisper:
"I am your Source."

This year, God taught me that provision isn't always about abundance, it's about alignment.
And alignment begins with obedience.

Recently, God instructed me to travel to Chicago for a private gathering of women I had never met. I went without knowing why. What I discovered was divine connection. We were not strangers, we were sisters, kingdom daughters, joint heirs, aligned without ever having crossed paths before.

Under the anointing of Makeda Smith and her wisdom circle, I listened to testimonies of women whose gifts had made room for them, sustained them, and elevated them. Their obedience became my activation. Their breakthrough awakened something in me.

In that sacred room, God spoke to me with unmistakable clarity:
"Fast. Pray. Prepare. Align."

And so, I entered this seven-day fast, not from a place of lack, but from a place of **expectation**.

I am fasting to make room for what God has already prepared.
I am praying to be found faithful over little so I may be entrusted with much.
I am preparing my heart, my finances, my home, and my

spirit for sustainable overflow.
I am aligning myself with the next dimension of my calling, where purpose is funded, gifts are activated, and divine order settles every chaotic place.

During this fast, I asked God to show me the blueprint.
And He did.

These seven days awakened truths I had overlooked about calling, stewardship, wealth, purpose, obedience, and the nature of divine provision. They reminded me that gifts are not optional. Gifts are assignments. When we pause them, everything connected to them pauses too.

This devotional captures the redirections, revelations, confirmations, and healing He gave me.
It captures the stretching and the alignment.
It captures the whispers and the warnings.
It captures the prophetic instructions for those called to more.

Above all, God revealed a truth He has been writing into my life for years:
"It's all connected."

Every sacrifice.
Every trial.
Every testimony.
Every delay.
Every door.
Every gift.

Every deficit.
Every miracle.
Every moment that carried you and every moment that stretched you.

All of it has been leading you here, to alignment and overflow.

My prayer is that as you walk through this devotional, your spirit awakens, your gifts stir, and your heart responds to God's voice with the same surrendered "yes" that transformed me.

This journey is not about lack.
It's about readiness.
It's about capacity.
It's about assignment.
It's about the God who restores, redirects, and reveals Himself even in the tightest seasons.

This is your moment to fast, pray, prepare, and align.
Welcome to your seven days of intentional transformation.

DAY 1

Your Gift Will Make Room for You

Scripture Focus

Proverbs 18:16 (KJV)
A man's gift maketh room for him, and bringeth him before great men.

Romans 12:6 (NIV)
We have different gifts, according to the grace given to each of us. If your gift is… use it.

Revelation Note

Unbeknownst to me, or perhaps perfectly aligned by God, my seven-day financial fast began on November 7th. The number 7 has followed me through every divine detail of this journey: the Chicago conference ($77), my flight cost ($77), and the host of the conference highlighting the number 7, and even referencing double 7's, each one a whisper of divine alignment and completion.

Scripture Reflection

When I first read Proverbs 18:16, I interpreted the "gift" as the talents God has placed within us, those abilities that, when used faithfully, open doors and create opportunity. But as I studied deeper, the Holy Spirit gave me a new perspective.

The Hebrew word for gift is **mattan (מַתָּן)**—meaning *a tangible offering, a present, or a token extended from one person to another.* That revelation shifted something in me. A gift doesn't just symbolize what we possess; it represents what we are willing to offer.

I began meditating on how my healing, leadership, and creative gifts already serve as keys unlocking divine access. I don't have to force doors to open; my preparation and obedience are what turn the key.

Personal Insight

The first thing that came to mind was my gift of holistic wellness advocacy and education. Through teaching, speaking, and mentoring, I share messages that equip others in mental, physical, emotional, environmental, and spiritual wellness. I do this freely, often pouring from a place of faith rather than surplus. Yet even in that, God reminded me that **my gift is a present, a tangible offering** that blesses others and simultaneously creates access for me.

My digital ministry, through social media, courses, and my business, has already been ushering me into rooms I once prayed to enter. I realized that my audience and ministry are not just assignments; they are avenues of divine provision. I had been thinking small, expecting a paycheck when God was preparing purpose-based profit.

Scripture Recall

Romans 11:29 (NIV)
For God's gifts and His call are irrevocable.

Even in moments when I've felt weary, unseen, or uncertain, this scripture reminded me that the call on my life has not expired. It simply waits for alignment, rest, and obedience.

Day 1 Journal Prompt

Question:
Where have I been forcing what God intends to flow?

Reflection:
Personally, I've been forcing my need for validation through certifications, degrees, and titles, chasing credentials when God was calling for consistency. My pursuit of yoga instructor, CPR instructor, and holistic nursing certifications are part of my preparation, but I've sometimes pushed for progress outside of divine timing.

Through this reflection, I realized that when things are truly aligned with God's will, they will flow instead of force. I am called to pray, fast, and prepare, not strive. As I continue to use my gifts in faith, I trust that they will make room for me according to God's plan, not my timeline.

Financial Reflection

Today as I was reading from the book *Making the Shift: From Self-Employed to Business Ownership* by Joy L. McLaughlin-Harris, I was challenged to examine what I'm willing to sacrifice for growth.

- I'm giving up mindless scrolling and replacing that time with meditation, study, and gratitude.
- I'm setting a weekly grocery budget and cooking at home to steward resources wisely.
- I'm identifying areas of emotional spending and realigning them with purpose.
- I'm saying no to overextending myself financially and yes to divine strategy.

I will be faithful in the little things, so I can be trusted with much.

Declaration of Alignment

"Lord, teach me to flow, not force.
Let my gift make room for me according to Your perfect will.
Align my timing with Heaven's calendar,
And let every seed I've sown in faith begin to bear fruit.
I decree that my preparation and obedience are opening doors now,
And that my gift will sustain me and glorify You."

Day 1 Summary

Today marks the beginning of divine preparation, a repositioning from striving to surrendered stewardship. As I align my work, my habits, and my finances under the authority of God, I'm learning that provision is not earned by effort but revealed through obedience.

This is not just a fast. It's a financial and spiritual reset. **My gift will make room for me, and my obedience will sustain me.**

DAY 2

The Irrevocable Call

Scripture Focus

Romans 11:29 (KJV)

For the gifts and calling of God are without repentance.

Revelation Note

God's promises are sure. He does not retract the gifts He has given or the callings He has placed upon our lives. His covenant is permanent; His Word will not return void.

We are accountable for how we use what He has entrusted to us, and our obedience determines how those gifts flow. The calling doesn't expire, even when our confidence does. It simply waits for our alignment.

Scripture Reflection

This verse reminds me that God's call is not conditional on circumstance. His covenant with Israel, and with all who believe, remains steadfast. God's blessings and callings are enduring, meant to bring glory to Him through our obedience.

No season, setback, or delay can cancel what God has spoken. **The call still stands.**

Meditation: Rediscovering My Calling

As I meditated on this truth, I reflected on how God has shaped my journey, the very steps that led me to discover my calling in nursing, healing, and holistic leadership.

Since middle school, I knew I wanted to be in healthcare. I loved learning, teaching, and comforting others. At nineteen, I became a nurse and quickly stepped into leadership roles. Early on, I recognized my gift for comforting patients and families, especially those walking through their most difficult days.

During my years in hospice, I learned that healing wasn't just about medicine. It was about presence. I remember one patient who was actively transitioning; I spent the day and night by her side, simply holding her hand, giving her daughter and family members a break from the shifts they shared keeping her hands warm. That was when I first understood the **power of touch**.

Later, I invited the patient's granddaughters to join me in moisturizing her skin, rolling her hair, and dressing her in her favorite glittery pink jersey and fancy jewelry. She looked like herself again. The family was deeply moved, and I knew then, my touch, my heart, my service, were part of my ministry.

Divine Continuation

Years later, my older cousin became ill with leukemia. She lived over three hours away, but God allowed me to travel back and forth to care for her. In those moments, I remembered the holistic practices that had once brought comfort: prayer, affirmations, breathwork, light movement, essential oils, and touch.

That season reignited something within me. I joined the American Holistic Nurses Association, studied integrative health, and attended holistic nursing conferences. There, God downloaded the vision for Precious Holistic Touch.

I began experimenting with essential oils and body butters yet fear and overthinking caused me to pause. The lack of validation from others who viewed these practices as taboo, truly made an impact on my insecure mind. I set budgets, created outlines, and made plans, but I never moved forward. That was in **2016**.

Now, in **2025**, I can see how God has redeemed that delay.

I'm walking in what was once only a dream, a nurse executive, licensed business owner, educator, nonprofit founder, and advocate for holistic wellness.

What I once saw as setbacks were actually **divine setups** for structure, clarity, and maturity.

Divine Alignment

Every detour, from hospice care, quality management, facility administrator, to holistic entrepreneurship, was preparation for this calling. God didn't remove my skills; He refined them for this season. The same healing touch that once comforted the dying now empowers the living.

Even when I doubted myself or paused in fear, the calling remained intact, quietly waiting for me to say "yes" again.

Prayer

"Father, reignite the vision You placed within me.

Restore my confidence in Your call.

Even when I feel weary or unseen, remind me that the call on my life has not expired, it simply waits for alignment and rest.

Teach me to respond with obedience and trust,

and let every gift within me glorify You."

Journal Prompt

What dream have I placed on pause that God is asking me to resume?

At first, I didn't have an answer, but as I prayed, God reminded me of my dream to complete my **Board Certification in Holistic Nursing**, a qualification that would open new doors for me as a subject-matter expert and educator.

This certification isn't about status, it's about stewardship, preparation, and readiness to walk fully in the calling God has placed on my life.

Wisdom Reflection

From *Making the Shift: From Self-Employed to Business Ownership* by Joy L. McLaughlin-Harris:

"Self-employed people don't own their business — their business owns them. If something happens to you, can your business continue without you?"

This question challenged me deeply. As the founder of my LLC and nonprofit, I realized that structure and delegation are essential for longevity. God showed me that it is not my employer that sustains me, **it is His glory that funds my assignment.**

Prophetic Reminder

While scrolling social media, I came across a post from Coach Jesse Cole (Founder of Kingdom Confidence) that said:

"Don't take a vow of poverty for the sake of holiness."

That statement resonated with my spirit.

I am not called to lack,
I am called to leadership.

Prosperity is not pride;
it's preparation for purpose.

Day 2 Summary

Day 2 revealed that God's call is not optional, it's eternal. Every experience, every pause, and every season of delay has been preparation. What I once viewed as unfinished work, God calls foundational training.

My assignment hasn't changed, only my readiness has.
The call remains.
Now, I'm answering it again with clarity, confidence, and commitment.

DAY 3

The Power to Create Wealth

Scripture Focus

Deuteronomy 8:18 (NIV)

"Remember the Lord your God, for it is He who gives you power to get wealth."

Revelation Note

It is not my employer who sustains me,
God funds my assignments.

I am not just building income; I am establishing covenantal wealth meant to sustain my family and the Kingdom. The wealth God entrusts to me is not a product of striving, but of **stewardship**.

Philippians 4:19 (NIV)

"And my God will meet all your needs according to the riches of His glory in Christ Jesus."

Reflection

When I opened my Bible to Deuteronomy 8:18, my attention was drawn to the importance of obedience. God was not speaking about achievement or hustle; He was speaking about **devotion**.

Every part of my being, my will, mind, body, and even my money, is designed to serve Him.

• My will commits to Him completely.
• My mind seeks to know Him through His Word.
• My body uses its strength and talents as tools of worship.
• My resources, finances, influence, creativity, are to be managed, not owned.

And then God reminded me:

"Do not become so busy collecting or managing wealth that you push Me out of your life."

This day's meditation deepened my understanding that wealth is **a covenantal exchange**.
It's not about accumulation.
It's about **access**, God granting divine strength, creativity, and strategy to those who steward His gifts well.

Meditation

Wealth is a covenant, not a coincidence.
When we honor God with our time, gifts, and obedience, He provides supernatural wisdom and divine strategy.

Prayer

"God, show me how to multiply what You've entrusted to me.
Thank You for the creativity that flows naturally within me.

Give me the strength and divine strategy to manage what I have now, so I can be trusted with greater abundance later.
You are my source.
You have given me the power to create and multiply my gifts to generate abundance.
Amen."

Divine Insight

While reflecting on yesterday's journal prompt, I realized that writing, poetry, and storytelling are gifts I unintentionally paused. But God is calling me to use them again, to speak, write, and teach through these gifts as **vehicles of divine wealth and purpose**.

These are not hobbies; they are **harvests**.

Practical Lesson: The Cake Moment

This morning, God gave me a gentle yet unforgettable reminder about discipline and obedience.

My oldest daughter came home from college and requested chocolate cake, so I baked one. The aroma filled the kitchen, rich and warm. I sliced two perfect pieces, ready to enjoy one myself.

Just as I was about to take a bite, the Holy Spirit whispered:

"You're fasting."

I froze, convicted yet grateful. I placed the slice back, covered the pan, and smiled. My daughter looked puzzled, she knows that chocolate cake is my favorite.

But that moment became a **teaching opportunity**. I explained to her that I am fasting, and during this fast, I am being fed by the Word of God. We talked about how fasting sharpens spiritual focus, strengthens discipline, and invites divine sustenance. I also made it my duty to explain to her that some things ONLY come through fasting and prayer.

Later, while preparing Sunday dinner, I felt the same temptation to taste-test. Instead, I asked my youngest daughter to read my journal reflections and affirmations aloud while I cooked. Together, we reflected on Scripture and the meaning of this fast.

God used that simple moment to show me:

Spiritual wealth begins with self-control.

Spiritual Truth

God is the giver of every spiritual gift and ability. He desires that we use them to edify His Kingdom and fulfill our calling. These same gifts open doors for divine connection, provision, and purpose.

When we follow His will, our gifts not only make room for us, but they also multiply.
And the wealth that flows from obedience is not just

financial,
It is **generational**.

Journal Prompt

How can I honor God as the source of my provision this week?
Reflect on practical ways to manage your finances, time, and talents as acts of worship rather than worry.

Declaration of Faith

"God, You are my source.
You give me the power to create wealth, not for status, but for stewardship.
Every gift within me is a seed of divine provision.
I will multiply what You've entrusted, walk in integrity,
and use every opportunity to glorify You."

Day 3 Summary

Day 3 was a day of revelation through obedience. From Scripture to the scent of chocolate cake, God reminded me that **discipline precedes abundance**.

True wealth is birthed in covenant,
in remembering Who provides the power, and why.

This fast is no longer just about finances,
it's about forming habits of holiness that lead to sustainable prosperity.

And through it all, God keeps whispering the same truth:

"I am your Source."

DAY 4

Established Work

Scripture Focus

Psalm 90:17 (KJV)

"And let the beauty of the Lord our God be upon us: and establish Thou the work of our hands upon us; yea, the work of our hands establish Thou it."

Revelation Note

This morning began with divine orchestration.

I woke up at 2:00 a.m., almost convincing myself that I had fasted long enough and heard enough from God, "Maybe I've received all the revelation, Maybe 7 Days is too long," I thought. But the Holy Spirit prompted me to join the 6 a.m. prayer call with Kendra Conyers. I hadn't joined in months, yet God drew me in precisely when I needed it.

As I logged on, I learned they were beginning a four-day fast, the exact number of days I had remaining in my seven-day fast. Instantly, I knew God was confirming alignment. I wasn't fasting alone; others in the Body were fasting alongside me.

Confirmation #1.

While on the call, I turned to my journal to take notes and it opened to an entry dated 5/22/25, about 6 months prior and the words stared back at me like divine timing:

"Some things come only through fasting…"

Confirmation #2.

In that moment, I knew I was exactly where I was meant to be. God was speaking, orchestrating, and strengthening me through obedience.

Prophetic Word

God whispered to my spirit:

"The gift and anointing I've placed in you will make room for supernatural increase and financial blessings. The communities you serve will learn of Me and build relationships while keeping their temples pure through holistic practices."

Confirmation #3 — the prophetic word sealing the next phase of my calling.

As I received it, gratitude poured from my heart:
"Thank You, Lord. Strengthen, encourage me, and send confirmation. You will never leave me nor forsake me."

Scripture Study Insight

My NIV Study Bible note for Psalm 90:17 reads:

"Because our days are numbered, we want our work to count — to be effective and productive.
We desire to see God's eternal plan revealed now and for our work to reflect His permanence."

That final phrase pierced my spirit:
For our work to reflect His permanence.

As one whose calling is to heal, teach, nurture, and serve, I realized that my work isn't meant to be temporary or fleeting. God is establishing **permanence**, work that outlives my hands and echoes His glory.

Meditation

Ask God to bless and stabilize your endeavors **so** they produce lasting fruit.

This morning, one word rose above all others:

STABILIZE.

God is not only blessing what we build,
He is rooting it so deeply in His will that it becomes self-sustaining.

For me, this means:

- Stabilizing my income and budget
- Establishing repayment systems for debt
- Rooting my business and foundation in long-term covenant

structure
- Becoming a **steward** of provision, not a **chaser** of profit

When we stabilize, God establishes.

Reflection

As I meditated, I realized this entire fast is about **divine establishment**, not human effort.

I prayed,
"Which projects or partnerships need divine establishment rather than human effort?"
and the answer was clear:
All of them.

My financial situation has stretched beyond human possibility. I've reached the place where only divine intervention can bring increase. But that is the exact place where God specializes, **in the impossible.**

This fast is not merely petition, it is surrender.
A spiritual document submitted before the throne of grace.
Not just for financial relief, but for wisdom, stewardship, and generational stability.

Covenant Prayer

"Lord, let the longevity and favor of Your hand rest upon everything You've called me to build.

Establish my work in permanence. not fleeting success, but eternal fruit. Let every seed I plant be rooted in righteousness, watered by Your Word, and multiplied by Your grace.
Connect me with mentors who are Kingdom-minded, stabilized, structured, and prophetic,
those who hear from You concerning business and financial matters. Breathe stability into my income, my ministry, and my foundation. And let Your beauty be upon the work of my hands."

Key Insight

When your calling aligns with God's purpose, **provision follows**.

Stabilize your systems.
Structure your business.
Steward your finances.

The blessing attached to obedience is **provision**.

Provision is not God merely supplying what you ask for,
It is Him **establishing what you were meant to sustain.**

Journal Prompt

Which areas of my life or work need divine establishment instead of human striving?
Reflect on where God is asking you to stabilize before He multiplies.

Write specific systems, habits, or partnerships that must be rooted for lasting fruit.

Day 4 Summary

Today was about divine confirmation and alignment.

God revealed that establishment is not just about structure, it's about stewardship with permanence.

He confirmed that my fast is not solitary but synchronized.
He affirmed that my calling is not random but rooted.
He reminded me that my provision is not limited but established.

Every confirmation today was God's way of saying:

"I'm building something through you that will outlive you."

DAY 5

Seek First the Kingdom

Scripture Focus

Matthew 6:33 (KJV)

"But seek ye first the kingdom of God, and His righteousness; and all these things shall be added unto you."

Revelation Note

Today's message came alive with deep conviction:

The "things" are additions, not the assignment.

When the Lord instructs us to seek first the Kingdom, He isn't only giving spiritual direction,
He's correcting our focus.

Too often, we pursue the "things": the outcomes, accolades, or affirmations… and call it obedience.
But the Kingdom is never built on results, it's built on relationship.

It's easy to assume we understand the assignment…
until we realize we've **overstood** it, standing *over* what God intended us to stand *under*.

When we overstand, we overlook the purpose… and idolize the results.

Scripture Reflection

As I prayed and reflected on the verse, God reminded me:

Alignment precedes abundance.

When the Kingdom is the priority, provision follows.

I revisited Psalm 90:17 from Day 4 and realized that the "work of my hands" is established not through human effort, but through divine order.

My responsibility is Kingdom work.
God's responsibility is provision.

The contracts, clients, increase, and resources are "the things" that God adds.
not the things I'm called to chase.

Meditation

"When the Kingdom is the priority, provision follows."

Sit with this question:

What if the overflow you've been praying for is waiting on your alignment, not your effort?

Pray:

"God, order my motives.
Let provision pursue me.
Teach me to seek Your Kingdom above every outcome,
so that everything You've promised can find me in alignment."

Personal Reflection

During this fast, God has been reshaping how I see my work.

I realized I had been trying to make my vision make sense instead of making it Kingdom-centered.

Before launching my business, I focused on material preparation,
buying supplies, designing labels, creating checklists, and setting up systems.

All good things.
But not **the** thing.

My notebooks were ready, but my **spirit** needed alignment.

Now, I understand:

The focus of the assignment is seeking God and building His Kingdom.

When I acknowledge that my calling is from Him and use my gifts to glorify Him, everything else is added.

Divine Realignment

God shifted my mindset today from **"building business"** to **"building Kingdom."**

He reminded me:

- The purpose of *Precious Holistic Touch LLC* is not profit, **its impact.**
- The focus of the *Foundation* is not visibility, **its vitality.**
- The goal is not to prove my ability, **it's to walk in obedience.**

When my motive aligns with His mission,
I become a magnet for miracles.

Prayer

"Thank You, Lord.
You've shown me that when I seek You first, You stabilize everything else.
I surrender every business, every plan, every idea back to You.
Let Your Kingdom come through my work.
Let my gifts be used as tools of teaching, healing, and restoration.
And let all the things, the favor, funding, partnerships, and opportunities,
be added unto me as I align my heart with Your will."

Action Steps: Realignment for Kingdom Focus

1. **Inventory your business motives.**
    - Ask: *Do these align with Kingdom impact?*
    - Remove anything that doesn't serve your divine purpose.

2. **Review your core values** for both your LLC and nonprofit.
   • Rewrite or reaffirm them so they reflect God's direction.

3. **Prepare the agenda for your next Board of Directors meeting.**
   • Begin with Kingdom focus, prayer, vision clarity, and value reaffirmation.
   • Ensure these updates are recorded in meeting minutes.

4. **Declare publicly:**
   "The motive of my work is to establish Kingdom alignment in all that I do."

Journal Prompt

How can I approach my business, nonprofit, or ministry decisions this week with Kingdom impact as the focus instead of outcome?

Write a short reflection identifying where your focus shifted toward "the things,"
and pray for realignment toward God's assignment.

Day 5 Summary

Today's revelation simplified everything:

When I make the Kingdom my priority, everything else finds its place.

The contracts, clients, and increase are not proof of success, they are fruit of obedience.

When the motive is pure and the mission is aligned,
God makes provision chase purpose.

This fast continues to remind me:
Alignment is the seed.
Abundance is the harvest.

Seek first the Kingdom,
and all these things will be added unto you.

DAY 6

Taught to Profit

Scripture Focus

Isaiah 48:17 (NIV)

"I am the Lord your God, who teaches you what is best for you, who directs you in the way you should go."

KJV:

"Thus saith the Lord, thy Redeemer, the Holy One of Israel; I am the Lord thy God which teacheth thee to profit, which leadeth thee by the way that thou shouldest go."

Revelation Note

This morning's focus was on **profit, not in numbers, but in purpose.**

The Lord whispered:
"I am your Teacher in all things that concern your growth."

Profit, in its truest form, is the *benefit of righteousness*, the outcome of obeying God's instruction and learning through His lessons. Every divine direction carries the potential for increase, but only when we follow through with diligence and humility.

As I reflected, God led me to another scripture:

Proverbs 14:23

"All hard work brings a profit, but mere talk leads only to poverty."

This reminded me that **effort and obedience are essential for fruitfulness.**

God mentors us through success and struggle, teaching stewardship, patience, trust, and spiritual maturity.

Prayer Reflection: Stewardship

As I prayed, one word rose above everything else:

Stewardship.

I reflected on recent spending decisions, purchases, payments, and withdrawals. Many were led by urgency, pressure, or emotion… not prayer.

If I had prayed first…
If I had waited for confirmation…
I could have saved stress, time, and money.

This was not condemnation.
it was gentle correction.
A reminder that God can only multiply what we manage well.

God impressed on me:

"Steward well over what you have so that I may trust you with more."

The true reward of stewardship is not money,
it is trust.
When God can trust you with wisdom, He can trust you with wealth.

Meditation

"God mentors you in success that glorifies Him."

Every season carries a classroom.
Even delays are lessons.
Even lack is instruction.
Even silence is guidance.

Meditate on this:

"God, what are You teaching me through this season of stewardship?"

Look for the lesson hidden inside the challenge.
Look for the wisdom tucked inside the waiting.

Personal Reflection

Over the last few weeks, I've been moving money across accounts, savings, checking, and credit, to cover my daughter's tuition and other needs. I prayed, fasted, and brainstormed ways to create income quickly through my business and nonprofit.

But God revealed something deeper:

**My lesson wasn't about money.
It was about trust.**

God's provision does not require my panic.

When I shift from striving to stewarding,
God steps in to multiply.

This morning, I wrote a new financial boundary, a covenant with God:

"I will make no decision that God doesn't get the glory from."

This is my new standard.
My new financial alignment.

Spirit-Led Revelation

God is teaching me a new dimension of success:

Spirit-led innovation.

He is teaching me to create from purpose, not pressure.
He is teaching me to produce from obedience, not urgency.

Profit will not be the proof of my effort,
it will be the fruit of my obedience.

Even my frustrations, the delays, the unmet needs, the unexpected expenses,
have been lessons in disguise.

God is building patience where I once sought instant results.

The truth:
Everything works out for your good when you steward God's lessons as carefully as you steward your income.

Prayer

"Teacher of profit, guide me in wise stewardship and Spirit-led innovation.
Help me recognize that every lesson, delay, and redirection is Your classroom.
I will learn, listen, and apply the principles of Kingdom stewardship.
Teach me to manage the small so You can multiply the greater.
May my profit bring You glory, not pride. Amen."

Life Application

- Before making any financial or business decision, **pause to pray.**
Ask: *"Is this aligned with God's purpose for my resources?"*
- Journal moments where God's timing protected or redirected you.
- Reflect on how waiting has revealed wisdom in past situations.
- Steward what's already in your hand before asking God for what's in His.

Journal Prompt

How is God teaching me to profit in this season, not just financially, but spiritually?

Write down one lesson, challenge, or decision that has matured your faith and improved your stewardship. Note how you will apply that wisdom moving forward.

Day 6 Summary

Day 6 brought correction wrapped in compassion.
God revealed that profit is not about accumulation,
it is about alignment.

Obedience produces overflow.
Diligence attracts divine favor.
Wisdom transforms lack into legacy.

As I prepare for the final day of this fast, I hold onto this truth:

**"God's hand teaches,
His timing tests,
and His trust rewards."**

DAY 7

Abundance in Every Good Work

Scripture Focus

2 Corinthians 9:8 (NIV)
"And God is able to bless you abundantly, so that in all things at all times,
having all that you need, you will abound in every good work."

God Is Intentional

From the very first day of this fast, God revealed His intentionality. Even the timing was divine.

When this fast began, my mind felt cluttered, my finances felt tight, and my faith in the area of provision felt stretched thin. I had been trying to make everything work in my own strength, shifting funds, crunching numbers, and striving to manage what only God could multiply.

This fast reminded me of a truth I had forgotten:

Some things only come through the obedience of fasting.

Even the number seven preached to me:
Seven days of fasting.
Seven months of financial stretching.
Seven signs of divine confirmation.

This was not coincidence.
This was assignment.

And when I said, *"I will fast for seven days,"* every pressure imaginable showed up at the same time:

- My graduate school tuition was due.
- My daughter's tuition, room, and board were due.
- My checking account had less than $100.
- My credit card was nearly maxed from covering essentials.

Yet, **I was not anxious.**
This fast was strengthening my faith at the very point where it had been trembling.

I refused to seek rescue from anyone else.
I did not call my "Superman."
I did not ask for help.
I needed God Himself to show me His power.

And just before 6:30 a.m. on the final morning…
my Early Pay Day hit my account.

I was able to cover the remaining balance for my daughter's spring courses to be secured.

God was not late.
He was precisely on time.

This Fast Was Always Meant to Become a Testimony

As I prayed, journaled, and obeyed God each day, He made it clear that this 7-day journey was not just for me, it was meant to free, shift, and align others.

This book is the fruit of His instruction.

Day 6 overflowed with revelation. God downloaded ideas, strategy, direction, and clarity, a divine setup for Day 7, the day of *abundance*.

And now, standing on the final day, I proclaim:

God is the God of the final hour.
He specializes in what seems impossible.

Reflection: Abundance Is Assigned, Not Accidental

God gives us abundance with purpose in mind.

Abundance is not random.
Not accidental.
Not earned by effort alone.

Abundance is assigned.

Assigned to callings.
Assigned to Kingdom work.
Assigned to those who steward well and obey.

God reminded me:

- Abundance belongs to the Kingdom.
- We are stewards, not owners.

- The authority to gather, manage, and distribute resources comes directly from Him.
- He blesses us so we can bless others.
- He provides for us so we can reveal what Kingdom provision looks like.

The true meaning of abundance is simple:

You have enough for yourself and overflow for others.

Meditation: Purpose-Sustained Prosperity

God whispered:

"True prosperity is purpose sustained by grace: enough for yourself and overflow for others."

Abundance is connected to assignment.

My nonprofit, my youth work, my advocacy, my leadership, my business, each is part of the "good work" God has entrusted to me. He showed me that my abundance is directly tied to:

- Raising holistically grounded youth leaders
- Supporting schools, guidance counselors, and families in need
- Standing behind the scenes as a vessel of healing and restoration
- Collaborating with administrators and community leaders

- Using my gifts to uplift the vulnerable and empower the next generation

This is the good work God is funding.
This is the good work I will abound in.

Prayer

*"Thank You, Lord, for more than enough,
enough to fund and fuel every good work assigned to my hands.
Establish the work of my hands and multiply every seed I sow.
Let my life be evidence of Your Kingdom abundance.
Amen."*

Journal Prompt

Where is God inviting me to expand generosity or collaboration?

Ask Him to highlight the youth, schools, community programs, or partnerships that are part of your Kingdom assignment. Write what He reveals, what stirs your heart, and what burdens refuse to let you go.

Closing of the 7-Day Fast

You did not just complete a fast.

You completed:

- A spiritual reset
- A financial recalibration
- A restoration of faith
- A realignment with calling
- A prophetic act of obedience

And the promise attached to your obedience stands firm:

"You will abound in every good work."

This chapter marks the end of the fast,
but the beginning of unstoppable provision, clarity, and alignment.

Closing Chapter:

Prayer • Reflection • Declaration
Alignment for Abundance

Waking With the Blueprint

On the morning of Day 7, I woke up with a peace so solid it felt like God Himself placed it on my chest.
I could feel it, He had given me the blueprint.

Not another budget.
Not another plan.
Not another scramble to "figure it out."

But a *blueprint of alignment.*

A whisper that said:

**"I will be your help.
I will be your provider.
You will see divine intervention."**

And as I sat in the quiet that morning, another voice rose in my spirit, the voice of my grandmother, Gloria.

I could almost see her in her white lace dress, cotton-candy-white nails shining under the church lights, singing with the choir:

"Order my steps in Your Word, dear Lord…
Lead me, guide me, every day

Send Your anointing, Father I pray…
Order my steps in Your Words."

What I didn't understand on Day 1 is what transformed me by the end of Day 7:
The increase is not the goal. The alignment is.

The financial breakthrough is not the evidence of success, *obedience is.* Impact is. Stewardship is. Purpose is.

For so long, I was moving. Busy. Budgeting. Creating. Organizing supplies. Drawing up capital plans. Doing all the right *tasks* with the wrong *posture*. What was missing was the one question I now ask before I make any move:

"Does God get the glory from this?"

Does God get the glory from this course?
This reel?
This product?
This caption?
This investment?
This photo?
This idea?
This partnership?
This purchase?

If the answer is no, I pause. Because I refuse to build anything that God is not breathing into.

During this fast, God said something to me so loudly that it shook me free:

"I am your Source. I will provide in ways that only I can get the glory for."

No loans.
No scrambling.
No forcing.
No surviving off hustle culture.

He reminded me:
"You are the lender, not the borrower. Walk in that."

And for the first time in a long time, I believed Him.

A Moment I Will Never Forget

As I mentioned in the early chapters, the morning during the fast, when I stood in the kitchen cooking with Emani, my oldest daughter. My youngest daughter Emily picked up my journal and began reading my affirmations aloud as I requested. There we stood… *three generations of purpose* in the making.

Emily reading.
Emani repeating.
Me echoing behind them.
The atmosphere shifting in alignment with God's perfect design.

It was that moment I realized,
This fast was never about money.
It was about **generational wealth.**
Generational mindset.
Generational healing.
Generational alignment.

God was using my obedience to reroute the inheritance of my bloodline.
My daughters were speaking declarations that would outlive me.

What God Delivered Me From

The panic of not having enough.
The fear of losing control.

The pressure of trying to be everyone's provider.
The anxiety that if *I* didn't make it happen, it wouldn't happen.

But hear me clearly,
I am not God.
I was never meant to be.

My job is alignment.
God's job is provision.

I learned that I can be a powerful nurse leader, a CEO, a mother, a partner, and a woman of purpose… and still be fully dependent on God.

This fast refined me.
It made me more grounded.
More discerning.
More confident.
More strategic.
More spiritually mature.

I am stepping into this next season not as a woman begging for a breakthrough,
but as a joint heir walking in my authority.

And I declare with every ounce of faith within me:

I WILL see the glory of God in the land of the living.
Not later. Not someday.
NOW.

Reflection

As you close this book, I want you to ask yourself:

- Am I aligned or am I just active?
- Am I busy or am I obedient?
- Am I surviving or am I surrendering?
- Am I praying out of fear or out of faith?
- Am I asking God for money or permission?

Because I promise you…
When you align your gifts with God's purpose, the blessings do not trickle,
they flow. Effortlessly.

The job is not your source.
The bank account is not your source.
People are not your source.
God is your Source.
God finances the assignment.
And **your calling does not expire.**

Closing Prayer

Father,
Thank You for every reader whose eyes have graced these pages.
Thank You for every tear shed in secret and every silent prayer they didn't have words for.

Thank You for the conviction, the clarity, and the confirmation You have poured into them.

Order their steps, Lord, just like the song my late grandmother sang:
"Order my steps in Your Word. Lead me, guide me every day."

Cover their families, their finances, their businesses, their health, their ideas, and their ministries.
Let alignment be their portion.
Let purpose be their compass.
Let obedience be their rhythm.
And let abundance be their inheritance.

In Jesus' name, Amen.

Declaration Over Your Life

Speak this aloud:

I am aligned.
I am called.
I am chosen.
I am provided for.
I am a lender, not a borrower.
I walk in purpose.
I steward well.
God is my Source.
Abundance flows to me effortlessly.
Generational wealth begins with me.

I will see the glory of God in the land of the living.
And I will finish every assignment God has placed in my hands.

Benediction

May your spirit stay open,
May your mind stay disciplined,
May your hands stay productive,
May your heart stay surrendered,
And may your life stay aligned.

May everything you release be rooted in purpose,
guided by faith,
and met with supernatural provision.

This is not the end of your journey,
it is the beginning of your alignment.

To continue your walk of holistic restoration, healing, and spiritual growth…

Visit www.PreciousHolisticTouch.com
Join our community, read the blogs, and enroll in the courses designed to nurture your mind, body, spirit, and purpose.

You are aligned. You are abundant. You are becoming.

Meet The Author

PRECIOUS DEAR

Nurse Leader • Holistic Practitioner • Founder • Author

Precious Dear is a Nurse Leader, Holistic Practitioner, and nearly twenty-year Registered Nurse dedicated to restoring wellness in the lives of individuals, families, and communities. With a blended background in clinical leadership and holistic care, she serves as both the CEO of Precious Holistic Touch LLC and the Founder of Precious Holistic Touch Foundation Inc., where she equips others with tools for mental, emotional, spiritual, and environmental healing.

Guided by faith and anchored in obedience, Precious has lived and witnessed the power of healing, alignment, and breakthrough in her own life. Her testimony is one of restoration through surrender, learning firsthand that when God orders your steps, overflow follows. Through seasons of sacrifice, caregiving, motherhood, leadership, and personal reinvention, she has embraced the truth that "It's All Connected." Every experience, every struggle, and every triumph becomes part of the assignment God has placed on her life.

As a holistic wellness advocate, Precious is passionate about transforming how people care for themselves, not only physically, but spiritually and emotionally. She empowers youth, supports communities, and uplifts families through education, mentorship, and intentional connection. Her work with the Precious Holistic Touch Foundation Inc. reflects her lifelong mission to cultivate healthy, whole, purpose-driven lives.

In addition to her professional and community impact, Precious is completing her Master of Science in Nursing Leadership and Administration, continuing her journey as a lifelong learner and servant leader. Her calling is woven through every facet of her life, mother, caregiver, mentor, nurse, and woman of faith, and her purpose is to create spaces where others can experience clarity, healing, alignment, and abundance.

Through her writing, coaching, teaching, and ministry, Precious reminds the world that God is still in the business of ordering steps, restoring hearts, and releasing overflow. Her life is a testament to the beauty of obedience and the transformative power of saying "yes" to God.

Connect with Precious

www.PreciousHolisticTouch.com

www.ingramcontent.com/pod-product-compliance
Lightning Source LLC
Chambersburg PA
CBHW040319170426

43197CB00021B/2960